Contents

Introduction: 15

Creating your signature colour: 17

Highlights: 23

All-over colour: 35

Guidelines for re-touching your roots: 43

Pricing story: 46

Jazzing up your blonde: 48

Top tips: 51

Why Blonde?: 58

Demystifying other colouring techniques: 65

Care for coloured hair: 69

Celebrity hairdressers: 77

Celebrity blondes: 79

Blondorexia: 112

London/LA/New York Blondes: 115

Power of the blonde: 126

I'm not offended by all the dumb blonde jokes because I know I'm not dumb... and I also know that I'm not blonde.

Dolly Parton

Introduction

I wrote *I wannabe Blonde* to give the client a much-needed guide to hair colouring. It is not for professionals, although that is not to say that they shouldn't read it. In fact, quite the contrary. The book explains the process by which one can achieve the different shades of blonde in the context of types of hair, claims on the client's time and, not least, cost.

When deciding to change or even just enhance your colour, there are several factors to take into consideration: you must ask yourself how much time you can devote to maintaining your new colour, what the cost would be, is your lifestyle going to affect the colour in any way. Going blonde can be low maintenance to high maintenance and if your goal requires you to go high maintenance, you might find that before long you have become a slave to your colour. If this is the case, you may start neglecting it – and looking it too!

There are other options available and you should get the best one for you, without being made to feel that you are getting second best. Once I have guided you through the maze of achieving a certain blonde, you may find that what you once thought impossible actually is possible.

To get the most from this book, you must first establish your natural base colour. The advice is of course no substitute for professional analysis but, in my experience, everyone knows exactly what their natural colour is.

Blondeness became a prejudice in the Dark Ages, an obsession in the Renaissance, a mystique in Elizabethan England, a mythical fear in the nineteenth century, an ideology in the 1930s, a sexual invitation in the 1950s, and a doctrine of faith by the end of the twentieth century. With its powerful imagery of wealth, light, youth, and vitality, built up over thousands of years, it has woven itself into the most popular materials of the imagination. In art and literature, in history and popular culture, blonde has never been a mere colour. For two and a half thousand years, it has been a blazing signal in code, signifying beauty, power, and status. From Greek prostitutes mimicking the golden haired Aphrodite, to the Californian beach babe; from pigeon dung and saffron dyes to L'Oreal-because you're worth it.

Joann Pitman

While we will be looking at products and techniques for lightening your hair, the final choice will be made between you and your hairdresser. That said, I have written this book for you, the client – not for the hairdresser – to give you a better insight into how to become blonde or blonder.

Even if you are already blonde, the book contains many great tips on caring for your hair and for livening up dull colour.

Definition of a blonde –
The definition of a blonde is someone who looks blonde.

A large percentage of people worldwide, however, interpret blonde as someone who has lighter hair. There is a category of people who do not think of themselves as blonde even though their hair has been lightened. Nevertheless they feel more glamorous with the lighter shade and in terms of salon colouring, lighter is certainly the more popular.

Historically speaking, this has always been so.

In all my experience with colouring hair, going lighter – whether or not it's intensely blonde, but just fairer – is still the one thing that gets the most attention.

Creating your Signature colour

Every woman is different in how she wears her hair blonde – some preferring softer lightening, others an extreme colour. The most common denominator, though, is that over time they tend to get caught up in the whole process and start requesting blonder and blonder hair colour. The direct result of this is going from low maintenance to high maintenance. Even if this does not represent a problem you must make sure, before you take the plunge, that you discuss this with your hairdresser, as your original maintenance programme will now change. When I explain this to my clients, sometimes they change their minds.

I am frequently faced with what I refer to as a 'lookalike blonde' – that is a woman who identifies with a celebrity and her shade of blonde hair and says to me, 'I wannabe like her.' While I have no problem with my clients going blonder, I do have one when they are copycatting some celebrity whose hair is probably nothing like it appears in the media. But in my hairdresser's chair the client is queen and if, after listening to me, they decide to go ahead, then I do my best.

Changing your hair colour dramatically can change your life and in some cases, I have felt that clients expected it. When the hoped for change fell short of their expectations, they felt disappointed. But such a change can have unexpected consequences: I have had clients whose partners develop a jealous streak as a result of a dramatic colour change.

free

Morocc...

Majiblond hi.B 92L con...
Majiblond hi.B 900s ana...

Remember changing your hair colour and even your life is not the same as changing yourself – that only comes from within.

While some people choose not to colour their hair, everyone can benefit from a little enhancement (as opposed to a dramatic change). Colour 'lifts' the hair up. Thus, a mousy blonde would look prettier with a few highlights in her hair.

There is a large percentage of women today who devote a great deal of time to grooming: hair is top of the grooming list and colour is top of the hair list. As the demand by women to have their hair coloured has increased, so have the products to do it.

Hair colour is very unique to each person and each person could have the most incredible and also, the most traumatic experiences with it. But when they've got it right... the feeling of gratification is amazing. All in all, changing one's hair colour can transform and boost your self-confidence .

Remember changing your hair colour and even your life is not the same as changing yourself – that only comes from within.

When people say the word 'blonde' they think of different shades of blonde hair. The spectrum of blonde is wide – from different levels and tones of blonde as in: medium golden blonde, dark honey blonde, light caramel blonde... and a woman needs to be within the spectrum of where her hair will look good and be easy to maintain. Today, with the help of make-up and advanced colouring technology, there is no reason why a larger percentage of women cannot be blonde.

Signature blonde...

...is what I refer to as the colour of blonde that you would most want to be and ultimately will wear. When you have this colour you feel your true self. Some people may cast a critical eye over your choice but it is the colour you most feel comfortable with. In achieving this colour, it is important that you change to your signature blonde with an understanding of what will be required to maintain it on a regular basis.

If your aspiration for a certain shade of blonde is not possible because of your natural hair colour or because you are not able to maintain the final colour, whether this has to do with the time or cost factor, then as sure as the sun will set your hair will take on the scarecrow look.

We have all seen examples of that.

My advice is: consult with your hairdresser and respect your limitations.

Where do I start?

How much time can you truly devote to your hair

colour? And how much can you afford to pay? Both answers will play a key factor in how blonde you can expect to become. You may find that it is possible to lighten your hair colour to a very light blonde but you may not be able to afford the cost to maintain this on a regular basis. Therefore, you may have to compromise for a more medium blonde that will cost less to maintain. Time will be another determining factor: ask yourself how often in any three month period are you prepared to sit in the hairdresser's chair and for how long.

It is crucial to remember that you will achieve better results in the beginning by using tint products to lighten the hair before you go on to using stronger lightening product such as bleach. Going straight to bleach on dark hair creates a worm-like effect and a very aggressive contrast in the hair.

The best blonde tones that are most complimentary to darker hair are light honey and soft gold and caramel tones.

Once you have identified your natural colour it will correspond with a number (see colour chart). This number will help you see the changes of level your hair will go through when you lighten it. Some natural hair colours are not suitable for lifting beyond more than 3 levels from their existing level. The book contains a pigment chart and to use it, it would be helpful if you have identified your level of lightness. If your hair colour contains more red pigment you will be more suited to the highlighting technique when going for the much blonder look.

When blonding brown and darker hair colour, the highlighting method is by far the most popular.

Colour Chart

10	LIGHTEST BLONDE
9	VERY LIGHT BLONDE
8	LIGHT BLONDE
7	BLONDE
6	DARK BLONDE
5	LIGHT BROWN
4	BROWN
3	DARK BROWN
2	DARKEST BROWN
1	BLACK

What are highlights?

Highlights are usually associated with very blonde hair.

Do remember that highlights are a technique and not a colour. Different colouring products and highlight styles can be used to achieve many variations of the colour blonde.

The basic principle of highlighting is when hair is woven, then the woven pieces are segregated from the rest of the hair and the colouring product applied.

What colourists use to segregate these strands from the rest of the hair will vary: foil being the most popular material of choice.

The weaves themselves can range from thick to fine and this will have a bearing on the final colour.

How light will my hair look when I highlight for the first time?

This will depend on the choice of colour used for the highlights and the style of highlights you have chosen.
On average, 30% of you hair will be coloured against 70% left natural – this is a good ratio to begin with, resulting in low maintenance. As long as the colours you have chosen do not contrast too heavily against your natural hair colour, you will not need to repeat this process again within a period of 3-4 months.

For women with brown and dark brown hair I recommend more honey and soft golden blonde highlights to begin with and for the first two times you highlight your hair. Trying to introduce very light blonde lights too soon against your darker hair will result in a worm-like effect.

If my hair is naturally darker does that mean I can never have very blonde highlights?

No, not at all. After a couple of applications of highlights, your hair colour will now take on a lighter look, roughly a dark to medium blonde. It is then that you can begin to introduce much

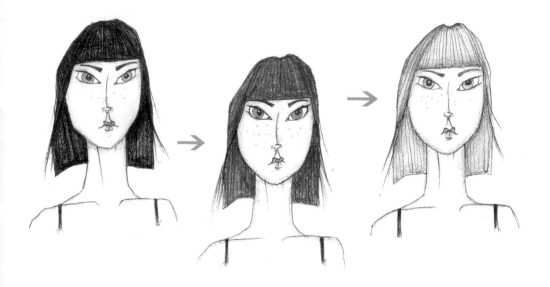

lighter blonde highlights to your hair as the contrast against your new colour will be softer and more flattering. Do bear in mind, however, that depending on how many highlights are introduced, your maintenance will increase from low to medium = 2 ½ to 3 months.

I would also point out that the percentage of hair that has been coloured has now increased on average to 50%. The increase will be more noticeable around the mid-lengths to the ends of your hair giving it a blonder appearance.

What happens when I am happy with the lightness of my hair?

From the moment you start highlighting your hair, your hairdresser may change the colour of your highlights each time you have them done. This may be at your request to achieve blonder hair. Once you are happy with the colour of you hair, your hairdresser will no longer need to add lighter highlights than the previous ones. The colour choice now will be made to maintain your signature colour. You can request to be put on maintenance colour on the 2nd or 3rd or even 5th application of highlights. The choice is yours.

If my hair is naturally blonde will I have to worry about roots as much?

Even with naturally blonde hair the highlights used will still have to be lighter than your natural colour, so depending on your colour choice your hair you will be governed by the same rules as those applicable to women with darker hair. Your roots may not be as visible but you will still have them nonetheless.
Women with naturally blonde hair will most definitely need to use lightening powder (bleach) if they wish to be much blonder.

Beware: excessive use could may result in your hair looking dry.

Once you have built enough colour into your hair using the
highlighting method and are happy with your signature blonde,
you must devote some effort to keeping the colour from changing.
Everyday shampooing and styling should only produce a small
amount of change over time and one that you would hardly notice
yourself. But taking your hair to warmer climes will certainly
change your colour, so as you would protect your skin, your hair
would need protecting as well to avoid any change. Blondes that
contain warmer tones are especially susceptible to sun
discolouration.

Just how much will my hair change in the sun?

This will depend on what products have been used to lighten your
hair and the percentage of your hair that is now coloured, and
how well you protect it from the sun. The larger the percentage of
natural hair colour left against the percentage that has been
coloured (your own natural colour will not lighten too dramatically
in the sun), the less sun discolouration will occur.
The reverse is true of someone who has a greater percentage of
colour.

*Naughty tip: If you do want
your colour to lighten a bit
a small exposure to
the sun will do this!*

What do I do if my colour lightens too much from the sun?

Next time you visit your hairdresser you will need to add reverse lights into your hair. These can be added at the same time as your re-growth highlights. Remember that it may take just a few reverse lights to solve this problem. Colours that are complimentary to the blonde hair should be used. Try to avoid colours that are too dark as the resulting contrast would only emphasise the blonde even further. A common mistake is to add a colour closely matching your natural hair colour, which – more often than not – is too dark.

Do I have to use bleach to lighten my hair?

No, not at all. There are other products that can be used to highlight your hair which can lift your natural base colour at least five shades lighter and will be kinder to the hair than bleach. High-lift tints can produce some beautiful shades of blonde and are

recommended for the more condition conscious women. Ladies with finer hair should try and avoid bleach – although they may be happy with the lightness they achieve, more often than not they will be left with poor quality hair.

My hair is curly and sometimes my highlights do not show, why is this?

Your highlights may be woven too fine and when the hair curls, the definition is lost and the end result is disappointing. You can either choose a thicker highlight or, in some cases, a slicing technique is recommended: this is when fine strips are used instead of weaves. You will find your end result will have much more definition than before, the definition can be made stronger by using blonder hair colour.

My highlights are beginning to look like an all-over colour. If I were to change to one, would my colour still look the same?

Changing to an all-over colour will produce a totally different colour than you get from a highlight, especially if you have been using lightening powder (bleach) to highlight your hair. You will

need a thorough consultation from your hairdresser before making a decision, another option, if you require less maintenance, is to tone down your existing colour.

My friend has her hair highlighted with quick mesh, she says this is better than foil. Is this true?

No, what you have to remember is that each hairdresser will have their personal preference as to what materials they use to highlight your hair. This has no bearing on the final result. I personally use foil or foam paper. You, as a client, may have a personal favourite, but pressurising your hairdresser into using a material that he is unfamiliar with could result in poor quality work.

IN THE SALON...

Yellow

ORANGE

To neutralise a yellow undercoat:
To neutralise an orange und
To neutralise a red und

When w

All·over colouring

Colouring your hair all over will, without question, produce an instant change. The degree of the change will depend on how much lighter you go from your natural colour. It is imperative that you get a thorough consultation from your hairdresser about the changes you can expect to see. You yourself must prepare for this change and be aware of what colour you can expect to see at the end. In all my experience, no matter how much I prepare my clients they are always surprised; therefore, you must allow yourself time to adjust to the change. This will have the biggest impact by far as it is instant and not gradual.

If your natural hair colour is light brown or darker, it is recommended that you lighten your colour no more than 3 levels up from its original level (see chart). Trying to go lighter more than the recommended 3 levels will produce a brassy looking blonde. This is because your natural hair colour contains red pigment (see chart). Once you have lightened your base colour no more than 3 levels, there is no reason why you can not have highlights on top of your base colour to achieve a blonder look without it looking brassy.

L'Oreal's MajiMêche is very good for this process and leaves the hair in great condition. Women whose colour is a natural dark blonde and lighter can achieve a much blonder all over colour with up to 4½ levels of lift from their original level colour.

The first time you colour your hair all over you will have to do what in the trade is called a virgin application. This can be a lengthy process

depending on the length of your hair. For future maintenance you will only need to do the re-growth, which is a much quicker process. How often you will need to repeat this will depend on the degree of lightness of your signature blonde.

Depth No.	Pigment
10	
9	
8	
7	
6	
5	
4	
3	
2	
1	

How often will I need to colour my re-growth?

Again, this will depend on how many levels of lift you have chosen as your signature blonde from your original hair colour (see chart).

Take this example: You are a dark blonde with a level lightness of 6, and you have chosen as your signature blonde a very light blonde, which has a level lightness of 10.

Consequently your hair colour would have 4 levels of lift (see chart). You can expect a high maintenance and will need to be colouring your re-growth about every 4 weeks. Signature blondes with only 2 levels of difference between their natural colour can expect in average to be colouring their re-growth every 4-6 weeks, but this may vary for each individual.

How many highlights can I add to my signature blonde?

There is no limit to how many highlights you can add, but remember the more you change your base colour using highlights the more this will change the over-all colour. Therefore, when you colour your re-growth to your original signature blonde, you may not get your perfect match with the colour as this contains no highlights. You may then need to add highlights to the freshly coloured re-growth to match the colour. While the end result can be quite stunning, be warned that this can become very expensive.

Another key point to remember is that longer hair when coloured all over will become much blonder over time through the mid-lengths and ends than shorter hair would. This would not be un-attractive as naturally coloured hair also gets lighter towards the ends.

My signature blonde is very light, at times I just feel it looks like one colour, is there anything I can do about this?

It is not uncommon for very blonde hair to look as if there is no dimension to it. You may consider adding some slightly deeper blonde tones to give the hair a more dimensional look. This is a very delicate process: if your colour choice is too dark they can produce too strong a contrast and look like worms in the hair. Additionally, the added dimensions may fade with shampooing and not last long in your hair.

One colour product that addresses all these problems and produces soft natural translucent tones to the hair is L'Oreal's Composite Colour. It is an amazing product and the only colour I ever use for this process when the signature blonde is this light.
Thank you, L'Oreal.

I'm not allergic to colour but find my scalp can be itchy when I have my roots re-touched, is there anything I can do about this?
I personally recommend that you do not shampoo your hair before you have your re-growth coloured. Try and leave it

at least two days prior to having them done, the natural oils from your scalp will help with this problem. You may rinse and style your hair beforehand but do try and avoid shampooing; if it persists, additives can be mixed in with your colour to reduce the itching in some cases completely.

I really like the lightness of my signature blonde but feel it is just slightly brassy, what do you recommend?

There may be 2 problems here:
1) your hairdresser might not be using the correct colour when lightening your hair to neutralise these brassy tones;
2) Your hairdresser may be lightening your natural base colour more than is recommended. If the correct colour is being used but your hair is still slightly brassy a few highlights may correct this. If this does not work you may have to consider toning down your existing colour.

What change can I expect if my hair is exposed to the sun?

Again, this will depend on the length of your hair and the degree of lightness of your signature blonde. But be warned, for very blonde hair this change could be considerable and its condition could also be dramatically affected.

If you have to expose
your hair to the sun,
protect, protect, protect!

L'Oreal Kerastase Soleil will meet all your hair needs while in the sun.
(By the way, I know I keep endorsing L'Oreal products but I do because, in my opinion, they are by far the best around. I am certainly not contracted to do this. My allegiance is to the client, not the company whose products I use. If another company began to produce better products, I would use them.)

I want to lighten my signature blonde all over, can my hairdresser change it?

Depending on how much you wish to lighten it, your colourist will have to choose a method, but you will most definitely have to lighten your existing signature blonde first in a very similar way to when you had your first time virgin application. When the new degree of lightness has been achieved your hairdresser will then colour match your roots to the new colour. The roots will have be re-touched much as before. The maintenance may increase for this new colour.

Guideline for re-touching your roots.

On average you can expect to colour your roots every 4-6 weeks, although this will depend on the individual themselves. I have some clients who are very blonde and very conscious of their roots and visit me every 2-3 weeks. They are usually in the public eye and, therefore, their hair is under much greater scrutiny.

Pre-lighten and toning

This is when the hair is pre-lightened first and a toner is applied afterwards. It is possible to lighten the hair up to 7 levels using this method from your natural colour (see chart). So for you ladies who have deeper hair colour and wish to be blonder this may be an option. Again, this does not come cheap and the maintenance is very high. Furthermore, this method still may not guarantee the signature blonde you are looking for.

Do speak to your colourist for more detailed advice of what you can expect to achieve. For all you light blonde ladies and up, you have the choice to become the *elitist blonde* as you are considered a perfect candidate for this method.

Gwen Stefani

Changing your existing base colour

If you already have your hair coloured using the highlighting method and are considering changing it, this should not create too much of a problem. Depending on your initial base colour this may be done quickly or over a period of time.

The number one problem I find with new clients is that their previous highlights have not been done very well and uncomplimentary colours have been used. The result being a mass of colour with heavy roots when growing out. Getting this under control is the first step. Nothing in relation to her hair bothers a woman more than feeling she has no control over her colour and is a constant slave to her roots.

Especially, if the end colour does not please her.

So using more complimentary colours to her natural colour, this may require some toning down of the old highlights or, at least, if the client wishes to remain very blonde, to ensure that the highlights are done in a more orderly fashion to allow for minimal roots when this grows out.

Changing the base of an all over colour may prove to be more difficult and will differ greatly from client to client. In some cases, the change may need to be executed at different stages over a period of time. Sometimes, it's not possible to change it instantly as one could when changing natural hair colour.

I remember the time Geri Halliwell paid me a visit in Manchester while on tour with the Spice Girls and asked me to change her colour to blonde. After explaining to her that this was possible, I told her it could only be achieved over a period of time, I said I could begin the process by removing the red from her hair that day. This would be the first stage in transforming her hair into a blonde.

A short time later she quit the group. Looking back, this was the first of many things that she changed. To distance herself from Ginger Spice, she chose her new blonde colour as a defining feature of this transformation. When I first saw her video, for her debut single with the coffin and showing Ginger Spice was dead, I was not surprised as many months earlier when I had coloured her hair, she had said to me, 'Get rid of this **** ginger!'

I was well aware then that she on the way to burying Ginger Spice.

Geri Halliwell

Pricing Story

In terms of paying for hair colouring, how much is too much or reasonable will vary from person to person.

The colouring rule of thumb: If you're truly happy with your colourist, then pay. Good colourists are more into the art of it than the money – they don't rip their clients off. But I would say that, wouldn't I?

I once had a client who was so cost-conscious about her hair colour that she pressurised us into putting highlights in her considerably dark hair at virtually apprenticeship rates.

One day she informed me that 'the hairdresser across the street said that he would charge me £50 less for a whole head of highlights'.

Enough was enough. I said I don't have to justify what I charge, but if she felt she could get the same standard of work, then it was her prerogative to change hair colourists. She called me six weeks later screaming that her hair had been ruined – that he'd made a complete mess of her hair and that it was awful.
She added, 'I suppose you're going to gloat and tell me, "I told you so."'

I replied, 'Certainly not. I'm going to tell you how much it's going to cost you to fix it.'

month 1 2 3 4 5 6

LOW

MED

HIGHLIGHTS maintenance

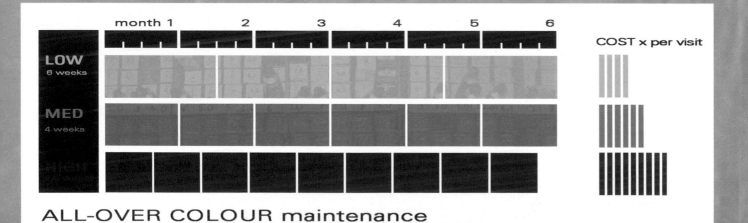

month 1 2 3 4 5 6

COST x per visit

LOW
6 weeks

MED
4 weeks

ALL-OVER COLOUR maintenance

Jazzing up your blonde

While a strong emphasis can always be placed on going blonder, women with medium to deeper blonde hair may prefer to jazz it up. This can be done by adding subtle or bolder slices to your signature blonde. These can range from soft toffees and caramels to strong coppers and even the odd light brunette. The spectrum is wide, the choice is yours.

Going blonde using the highlighting method

 When using this method to go blonde, the cost and time to achieve your signature blonde will depend on how much lighter your signature blonde is from your natural base colour, this being your starting point. Taking into account that complimentary colours are used to lighten your hair at each stage of each highlight application. The first time you have your hair highlighted you can expect to see a noticeable difference, yet most of my clients want to be blonder still.

This process of colouring the hair will enable your hairdresser to produce slowly but surely a controlled and natural blonde look over a period of time. Your hair will gradually evolve into your signature blonde. I refer to this as blonde evolution. Trying to overload the hair with highlights on the fist application will result in a higher percentage of coloured hair too soon and in a heavy re-growth. You want the percentage of colour to build in the hair around the mid-lengths and ends. This will happen naturally over 2-3 applications even when a small percentage of highlights is added each time.

Overloading the hair with highlights will only result in a revolution. After the second application of highlights, the hair will be noticeably different. Also, a three month period will have elapsed since your first application of highlights. During this time the first set of highlights may have even lightened due to the everyday elements hair has been subjected to. At this stage you may choose just to maintain the colour you already have.

Time factor for this – 9 months
Cost per application of highlights x 3 = final cost. Maintenance: low.

If you choose to carry on, your time scale will become shorter between applications and you would have your fourth set of highlights at 2½ months, as you are now going blonder. You may now want to consider introducing much lighter blonder tones to your hair. You may choose to stop at this stage.

Time period – 14 months
Cost per application of highlights x 5 = final cost. Maintenance: medium.

If you choose to carry on you will most definitely be going into very high maintenance, but the end colour will be unquestionably blonde.

Time period – 19 months
Cost per application of highlights x 7 = final cost. Maintenance: high.

You think Jennifer Anniston did it over night? I don't think so!

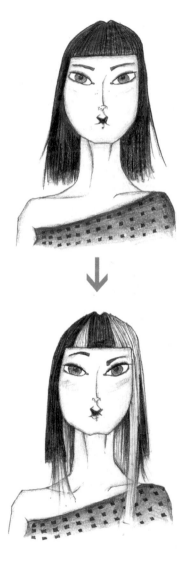

Rocket Blonde

Time has become very precious for us all, so sitting for hours at a time having your hair coloured is not an option. Most clients want quick instant results and therefore some colour products have been developed to address the demands of time conscious clients. L'Oreal's LUO colour is one such product and has a selection of blondes that can lift your natural base colour 2½ levels in twenty minutes. This can be used to create quick soft natural highlights to your hair. Alternatively, it can be used for all over colouring. The consistency of this product on a professional level allows for a speedy application and also contains grapeseed oil that adds incredible shine to your ends' colour, and boy, does it shine!

Not forgetting highlighted ladies, L'Oreal also have a product called MajiMêche that can lift your colour up to 4½ level in fifteen minutes when processed with heat. Ideal for quick pick me ups for blonde-haired ladies when feeling a little dull.

The cost – getting it right

There are two ways of going about this. Firstly, you can take a look through the glossies to see what colour you most would love to be, regardless of any idea of the cost factor to achieve and maintain it. Take the pictures along to your hairdresser and get a breakdown of your choices and, if possible, how long will it take you to become your signature blonde. If you find this over-budget, you can always start at the other end: tell your hairdresser your budget for colouring your hair and the time you can devote to maintaining it, then you choose.

Top *TIPS*

* When you are having highlights, it is important to remember that thickness or thinness of the weaves will vary, because hairdressers work differently. It is important to address this when you speak to your colourist and be very specific about your preference. Sometimes certain shades may need to be picked up with a stronger thickness of highlight.

* Chunky does not necessarily mean stronger contrast. This would depend on the colour used against your natural base colour.

* Hairlines and partings: If you are on your darker side and have started to achieve the blonder look that you're going for, yet you still feel you want some extra blondeness, it's best that fresh highlights are put in under the parting and away from the hairline because it will create less contrast as they grow out but will still be visible.

* The myth about always wanting to have a few blonder highlights around the face. More often than not, to achieve this your hairdresser will use a bleach. They have to be careful, because this hair tends to be the finest and most fragile and this can be stressful to the hair, even resulting in breakage. I personally prefer to use a tint product, which is much kinder to the hairline, when highlighting.

* Top professional tip for the girls whose highlights are dulling: after a while, the highlights themselves are going to get muddy through pollution, products, swimming, etc., – all this has a dulling effect. My suggestion for shining stars who are feeling a little tarnished is to give your hair a good cleanse. As the elements from every day living have basically started to dull the hair, a client will often say they want more highlights. What they don't realise is that the their colour hasn't changed, it's just been covered by a dirty film.

* L'Oreal have a fabulous professional process called Gentle Cleansing which will basically take you back to your original blonde without ever having to put a single highlight into your hair: it freshens your hair making you a shiny, sparkly star again. After all, just as the skin gets dull, so does the hair.

Top TIPS

* Colour shampoos and conditioners are a good way to keep your colour looking its best between visits.

* Do try and get your hairdresser to customise your favourite conditioner to really compliment your colour better.

* Warmer tones around the face for grey-haired clients while flattering can sometimes make you feel not quite as blonde as you would like. Adding a few blonder lights and sitting them behind your warmer tones and away from the face will give you that much needed lift you are looking for.

* If looking at the same colour day in and day out you get bored and not see it for its true colour, you may be in blonde denial.

Do get hold of a cheap brown wig and wear it around the house for a day, periodically looking in the mirror. When you take it off you may find that the colour you where thinking of changing to is the colour you already are

* Really want a blonde boost to your colour without the roots?

Do try adding blonder ribbons to your hair – these can be done in various styles to suit your own taste. The colour is applied at the mid lengths to the ends, staying away from the root, giving a much needed lift with no extra maintenance.

* Do try to avoid tipping just the ends as this can sometimes make the ends look dry and give the appearance of growing out an old colour or, God forbid, of neglect.

* Do remember that hotel pools can play havoc with very blonde hair, changing the colour to all sorts of greenish hues. Don't panic! I have a fabulous quick fix solution to help with this, but again results may vary from person to person. Try putting tomato ketchup in your hair, massage gently into the greenish hues, on average twenty minutes – this should alleviate the problem.

Failing that, there is a clarifying gel that is especially designed for this problem and it works – it is also very condition friendly. Not all hairdressers stock this, you may have to phone around, but it is out there. Alternatively, you can find details on **www.shaunpulfrey.com**. Whatever you do, avoid letting your hairdresser bleach this out as your colour will change and the condition of your hair may be seriously affected, too.

✳ ❋ ✳

Top TIPS

Why Blonde?

Do blondes have more fun? No, not necessarily. I don't think they have any more fun than anyone else. But in terms of glamour and what is instantly sexy, blonde is the colour. Look at the way Marilyn Monroe and Jean Harlow, the blonde bombshells of the last century, were marketed. Their image was created by the film studios and once it struck gold — well, in this case, blonde — it never changed. Clever advertising knows its blondes.

Budgeting

Super high-maintenance scenario:

Super-high maintenance hair is not an issue for either the rich client or the one whose income depends upon the blonde bombshell look. The issue with them is getting the right person to do the job on time. The problems occur when the client wants super-high maintenance hair on the cheap and starts to cut corners, such as having her roots done every four weeks instead of three. It doesn't work. She will look better and be liberated from being a slave to her hair colour if she tones down her colour to what she can afford. Her colourist will appreciate it, too.

Good colourists want the client's hair to look its best before they want her money. Colouring is not a trade or a craft, it's an art and, while artists are not above money, it is secondary to their work.

In conclusion and based on what we've already discussed: choose the colour that you would like (or how light you would like your hair to be) carefully. Find out what it will take to get there, and see if the cost and maintenance factors fit into your lifestyle and your budget. If they don't, then you reconsider your colour.

Going blonde on a budget

These are clients who go to the hairdresser twice a year. A typical budget blonde is one who wants to see some colour in her hair, but doesn't want the maintenance. She wants to have the colour grow out of her hair without having to maintain it.

You can put highlights into the hair, but very sparsely so only 10% of the hair would be coloured. I would not recommend going lighter than 3 levels of lift from your original base colour. You may also want to consider that these highlights will naturally lighten over time, depending on the elements you subject them to. This may have a bearing on the choice of your colours. Maintenance: zero. You could consider one application of balayage (see p. 65).

For a more customised personal signature look you could choose to add segments of blonde to your hair, as few as 3 or 4. As long as these are hidden away from your parting and hairline, there will be no reason why you could not blonde them considerably. Although the re-growth would appear, it would not be visible to the naked eye unless you were to part the hair and look for it. Maintenance: zero.

Carrie, from Sex and the City, for example, did this very well, having segments of blonde - selected pieces in the hair that were, in fact, very blonde. Her hair is very curly and when blow dried straight, it took on a different appearance from when it was all messy and curly, but you could actually pick the section of the hair that had been blonded. These segments are done away from the root area, away from the partings.

This is a style that can be very low maintenance, because it doesn't involve a uniform colouring such as all-over blonding. The process allows for more contrast in the hair.

And because there's a good 85% left of the natural hair colour, and because the colour added to the hair is not uniformly woven, this will reduce any contrast when the hair begins to grow.

It is, therefore, important to invest in an excellent hair colourist and explain what your priorities are.

By the way, no top professional hair colourist looks askance at a client who lays her financial cards on the table. Faced with this situation, I always consider it a challenge to create a colour for a client and a plan that fits into her particular budget or lifestyle.

Going blonde on a shoestring

This is for people with ultimate limitations who cannot afford salon visits at all.

If you fall in this category, your best option is to find a good salon that offers complimentary consultations and explain what you want to achieve and what your constraints are. You might lie a little, if you must (go on), and not actually admit that you propose to colour your hair yourself.

Do find a salon/hairdressing school that constantly requires models for colouring services for their trainees. You will also receive professional advice on hand from the instructors themselves. There is a small cost for these services. In some cases they are complimentary.

Do call free call numbers on all hair products if you must colour your hair yourself. They will advise you on the best product to use for the result you require.

Do make sure that you are not caught up in a wave of publicity that is targeting you as a customer.

Do discuss the colour and condition of your hair honestly, so that you would receive optimum advice. It is important to exhaust all avenues of research and get plenty of advice before embarking on a DIY method.

There exist on the market highlighting kits that allow you to paint the colour on to lighten your hair. The rule of the thumb is to be careful with the roots – it is always better to highlight the mid lengths to ends, so as to give the impression of sun-kissed hair as opposed to concentrating heavily on the roots which could produce patchy results for the inexperienced.

There is a degree of skill involved in using home highlighting kits that require freehand painting. Therefore, to reduce the risk of a catastrophe, it is sensible to practice beforehand. Try using hair conditioner instead

of the actual hair colour. When you feel confident enough, then use the colour as per manufacturer's instructions.

Do remember that less is more: if you are new to this, read carefully, think carefully, and perhaps reduce the amount of colour going into your hair to begin with. If it is successful and you like it, you could always add more in later.

Do remember that going blonde will be permanent – it will not wash out. Lightening your hair is a choice you have to live with long-term. Even if you change back to your original colour, the condition of your hair could be affected dramatically and it will not be the same until all the evidence has been removed – either by cutting it out or growing it out.

De-mystifying other colouring techniques

Balayage

Balayage is a method of colouring where the colour is applied free hand to the hair. As with all colour, the final result will depend on what your hair colour is before the application – whether it is natural or already coloured. It can produce some great pick-me-ups to already blonde hair and soft warm tones to dull looking blondes. This method requires a great deal of skill and, as with all colouring techniques, has its pro and cons.

I have corrected quite a few heads of hair in my time when this method has been used over a period of time to create a natural looking blonde. Where a hairdresser is very heavy handed over, probably, 3 to 4 applications, the client ends up looking like an all-over colour with very heavy roots apparent. In this scenario, re-touching the roots using this method, a lot of colour overlap is produced, creating very dry and over processed hair.

Consequently this would not be my personal recommendation for building controlled colour into the hair when going blonde.

Like all methods of colouring the hair, if executed badly or is not suited to your hair, the end result is obvious. Do make sure you get proper and comprehensive advice before choosing this method.

Smudging
(lightening your natural base)

Another method to consider is smudging – a tint is smudged into the hair and processed for a shorter length of time (approximately 10 minutes). Depending on your natural base colour, this would lift it slightly producing light golden tones. Highlights can then be added and this can certainly help build up the evolution process.

Do consider, though, that highlights might not lighten up as well as if you hadn't had the smudge. This is because the hair has already been through a colour process at the time of highlighting the hair.

Do also consider that hair that has been through a colour process would be more susceptible to the elements – from everyday styling to extreme cases when the sun changes the colour from its original colour, occasionally producing a more rooty look as it begins to grow out.

I sometimes suggest a partial smudging staying away from partings and hair lines and hiding the smudge. Highlights can then be added through the partings and hairline to marry them all together eliminating any heavy root grow out (this may occur if the smudge lightens in time).

Do note that when the smudge lightens you will lose the highlight definition that you had in the beginning. Do make sure you are aware of what will be happening to your colour in the future as it goes through the elements of your life style.

Colouring Grey hair

More and more of you are becoming greyer at a younger age. Do not panic, however.

There are so many techniques to blend and marry grey with your colour when going blonde that there is no need to dash straight for all-over colouring.

Do talk this through with your hairdresser as every case is different. Now, the bright side – and yes, there is one: if the percentage of grey becomes greater than what is left of your natural hair colour, the red pigment, which would have been present in your natural hair, will no longer be there. Thus, the most troublesome problem to going blonde, is already solved.

> **And you actually have a greater choice of blonde shades. This is one grey cloud that definitely does have a silver lining (I could not resist reworking the old cliché).**

Grey hair comes in all forms, some even very patchy. If your newly grey hair is patchy, your hairdresser can come up with various options for you.

Sometimes, blending the grey in with highlights may no longer be an option as the grey will still dominate in appearance when finished. Whether this option is suitable for you is down to individual choice.

When having a tint to cover the grey, the same colour may not be suitable for what is left of your natural colour. This may result in areas of patchy, brassy blonde. I have come across this many times with new clients, yet a simple solution is at hand.

Do ask your hairdresser to use two different colour tints to achieve one even colour or as close to it as you can get.

I am not being holier-than-other-colourists for pointing out that, when going blonde, women with grey hair are often badly served.

The main issue, from the client's point of view is to cover the grey. Once it's gone, she tends to be so pleased that she remains unaware that much more can be done to really bring out the best of the hair colour.

> ***Do bear in mind that***
> ***lighter hair is more flattering***
> ***yet can also look flat***
> ***with no dimension to it.***

I often use a free hand method to put dimension into my clients' colour, using complimentary tones to their tint. This takes no more than an additional 5-8 minutes once the tint has been applied to the roots.

Do not feel you have to pay a million dollars to look it.

Care for **coloured** hair

You've already spent a great deal of money having your hair coloured. Using the correct shampoos and conditioners to maintain your colour at its best is imperative. Harsh shampoos may even affect your colour, stripping out, over a series of shampoos, your soft delicate tones that my have been added to your hair. There is no reason why you cannot find a shampoo that will also meet your hair's texture and your scalp's needs as well as being colour-friendly.

Do remember that natural oils will only build up on the scalp and, therefore, when shampooing you need only apply product to the scalp itself.

Do not put a lot of shampoo through the lengths of the hair – as this travels down your hair from the scalp, it will clean it sufficiently without scrubbing and agitating.

Do squeeze out the excess moisture, then use conditioner in the ends of the hair. The conditioner is dispensed into the hands and applied to the ends and then worked up into the hair.

Do not pour products directly on to the hair. Rather, dispense products in the palms of your hands first, then distribute over the hands and transfer evenly to the hair.

Do start combing at the ends, not at the roots – most people dig the

comb straight in, that will actually lock the knots already in your hair. Conditioners do vary in quality – the cheaper brands tend to be heavier and greasier. The L'Oreal Kerastase brand is of salon quality and achieves best results.

The only product that goes on to the roots is shampoo. Conditioner is very rarely applied into that area. Hair at the roots tends to be the strongest and newest and, therefore, gets a lot of natural oils coming from the scalp.

How often to shampoo?

Many women wash their hair every day – and not necessarily because it's dirty. It has more to do with lifestyle habits.

Do just rinse the hair through, if you feel you need to wash it or shall we say style it. Sometimes you may find that it is easier to style your own hair when it's not freshly shampooed.

Do not massage or rub the scalp vigorously as this stimulates the sebaceous glands and makes your hair oily. People who have a tendency to greasy hair need to be gentle at the shampooing stage. On the other hand, dry hair benefits from scalp massage.

Blow-drying time

When it comes to bad hair days, it is usually their blow-drying technique that lets people down.

If you overdo it, the hair gets static and starts flying away. If you leave it that little bit damp (and it is easy to misjudge this if the hair feels dry), it retains some moisture and later flops. Finishing products won't be effective because your hair was never finished in the first place. It's all about getting the right balance.

What products

Don't let the vast multitude of products confuse you.

Do consider whether you may already have the product you are being sold at home. Responding to different packaging or clever marketing doesn't just burden your budget – it makes you use excessive amounts of the same or similar products on your hair.

Do sit down and work out what you need for your hair? Your hairdresser would be more than happy to help.

Straight smooth hair will reflect the light that will create shine. On hair that is slightly more wavy, you will need a serum to actually help give this illusion.

If your hair is curly, it may sometimes be better to use a gloss spray that will help reflect the light.

Changing products every now and then can be beneficial for getting the build-up out of the hair. The major benefit, however, is psychological: *If I change the product, my hair would get that much shinier.*

In this day and age, there's very little by way of build-up in the hair that basic shampoo does not remove. Contemporary products aren't meant to be heavy and stick around in the hair. The biggest build up on the hair comes from the impurities in the water. A basic mild shampooing would take that out. I think product build-up may be something that's been perpetuated through the myths of the industry itself. Most products are soluble and wash out easily.

If you live in an area where the water is heavily mineralised, this can produce deposits on your hair that may not be visible to the eye, but will have a dulling effect on your hair. There is gel cleanser for removing these elements, bringing the shine back in your hair.

This is more pertinent to blondes as dulling and build-up result in an actual change of colour. Brunettes suffer from build-up in the hair, but the dulling effect is not obvious.

Natural products

Do not bother smothering your hair with edibles such as egg, yoghurt, vinegar, etc. Their molecular properties are not powerful enough to penetrate into the hair, so this is a waste of both time and produce. All they do is coat the hair.

They do not harm the hair, but the benefits are largely psychological. The advances L'Oreal have made with their hair care range are far more beneficial than any of the more natural products would be.

Do work out which products are suitable for you before buying. A gentle shampoo that doesn't strip the natural oils would clearly be preferable. For coloured hair, conditioner alone may not be enough – a finishing product may also be required after styling, such as a serum.

I suspect women enjoy putting different products in their hair, because it makes them feel that they are doing something special.

Do bear in mind your own hair limitations when trying out new products.

Do not expect to end up looking like the model on the packaging.

More often than not, the models whose pictures you see on the boxes have the natural colour they are marketing. A natural redhead being chosen to market the red and the blonde, more often than not, is a natural blonde.

Even though it is against advertising regulations to use such methods to advertise colouring products, these regulations are impossible to enforce.

The marketing people choose the girls who have naturally got the colour that is being advertised as coming from the packet.

So before you even start to emulate the picture on the package, the odds are stacked against you.

Years ago, I was commissioned to colour the models' hair to appear on the boxes for a colour brand manufactured by Wella. Therefore, I know what happens.

Celebrity Hairdressers

Having a client base that reads like *Who's Who* helps establish a high profile salon, as does a good PR. Another hugely important element is having a strong business partner.

Nicky Clarke has his wife Leslie and Richard Ward has Helen – these are the movers behind the scenes, while the husbands get on with the creative side of hairdressing.

In my professional life I have worked for a number of famous hair salons in *the* locations: from Rodeo Drive to Sloane Street, via Fifth Avenue and Mayfair. By the way the Mayfair client will always remain in Mayfair and tends to rotate amongst the neighbouring salons.

Nicky Clarke has long held a special position in the hearts of the British media and is quoted more frequently than any other hairdresser. Everybody who was anybody in the '80s and '90s has been through his salon.

Jo Hansford, best known as a hair colourist, worked for Daniel Galvin before opening her own salon. Her particular claim to fame is colouring The Duchess of Cornwall's hair the day before the royal wedding.

Michael John, John Frieda and Vidal Sassoon were established well before anyone else and of the two, John Frieda is, today, more associated with hair colouring. Sassoon's has long been the leader amongst hairdressers for innovative and creative ideas.

John Frieda didn't have his products line or anything like the notoriety he now enjoys when I began my career. He was cutting hair, quite simply. In any case, there weren't really any celebrity hairdressers at the time.

I work at Richard Ward's salon, which has the very solid history of being *the* Sloane Street salon. His early clients were not as famous as they now are, Tara Parker-Tomkinson being a good example of the loyalty they show him. His award winning London salon in Sloane Street is now a Mecca for celebrities such as Liz Hurley, Trinny and Susannah, Will Young and Sophie Wessex. Richard's hair attitude is about making women feel beautiful – his signature look is sexy, glamorous, wearable hair.

Celebrity Blondes

Victoria Beckham

I first met Victoria when she had just started dating David. I had been asked by a friend to colour her hair on a regular basis at David's home.

At that time Victoria was very interested in David becoming blonder and having highlights in. He did end up having his hair highlighted and going quite blonde, but much later. As for her, she too went blonde later when her hair was very very short, but it wasn't very successful.

Around this time, Victoria did something for me that was extremely kind and for which I am still grateful.

A friend of mine who has Down's Syndrome called Lee was a huge Posh Spice and David Beckham fan. I told Victoria about him and asked her if she would sign a little photograph. She asked me to invite him to David's house there and then.

David was at football practice and had no idea what was happening.

We'd just finished doing her hair in the kitchen and it was about 12 o'clock when the doorbell rang. Before Lee's arrival, I said to Victoria, 'After meeting you, he may not want to leave, so when we've had enough I will say that you've got to go on a plane and that you've got to go see Sporty Spice and that way round he'll have to leave.'

The doorbell rang, it was Lee, with his mother. I still remember him at the door – he'd got a little bunch of flowers that he'd picked. At this point Victoria came out of the kitchen and exclaimed, 'Oh, is that Lee?' He ran over to her, yelling 'I love *yous*', dancing and singing. She was incredible, the way she made a big fuss of him.

And then through all this commotion going on in the kitchen, in walked David, and there was Posh Spice with Lee running round his kitchen. Lee started screaming again, 'Oh, you scored that goal', jumping about because his idol was David Beckham as well.

They were absolute sweethearts until I started going, 'Oh, we've got to go now Lee, Victoria's got to get on a plane to go see Sporty Spice.'

David looking nonplussed, 'What, where is she going? Who's going where?' He didn't get it and Victoria rolled her eyes. But they absolutely made Lee's Christmas.

Today, Victoria's hair is very long, but helped by the high quality hair extensions. She has turned to hair extensions for her image even sometimes choosing to have blonde extensions added. In true Victoria fashion she carries it so well.

> *My personal take on hair extensions is that they can be great fun giving you an instant change of your hair length and of course, your colour.*

Now hair extensions can be great fun, giving you an instant change of hair length and, of course, colour. In many cases, taking you into a zone your own natural hair could never go. However, when very long hair extensions are used, an incredible amount of stress is put on one's own natural hair. In extreme cases, this causes a condition known as female pattern baldness. The head, while not totally bald, looks like the victim has undergone chemotherapy!

A few placed in the hair here and there to pick it up a little is great. I just get a little concerned when someone comes to rely on them so heavily for their image. This then becomes a self-perpetuating thing to the extent where they can no longer take the extensions out for fear of appearing bald. So, my advice is to get all the facts before embarking on using hair extensions. Short-term use seems to have less effect on the hair, as long term use will have.

Victoria Beckham has used hair extensions for a number of years now. I believe that were she to take the extensions out of her hair, apart from her hair being very much shorter, it would most certainly be much thinner than when she started having extensions.

Nancy Dell'Olio
Hair extensions addict – is almost certainly balding, as a recent photo shows.

The funny thing is, it has often crossed my mind how David might feel about someone else's hair on his wife's head, lying next to him in bed. Little did the woman who sold her hair in the first place ever imagine that her hair would be lying next to David Beckham.

Sharon Stone She's another one who sold 'the dream' so very well, even though it was very short-lived. These people do have bad hair days, just like everyone else, but most of the time when you do see them, it's at a premiere or some glamorous event when the hair, of course, has been very, very well groomed. I think Sharon Stone has the stuck-to-her-head hair syndrome just as many ordinary women do. When she came out with that short blonde hair, many women would have liked to followed suit, but the high maintenance such a style demands would have put them off.

Keira Knightley

She's a very pretty girl. And with a pretty face, who can take a colour change more often than not. We've already established that going blonde is a much more acceptable change and that most skin tones can take it.

For me, the hair cut is too short to even begin to show tonal blondes in the hair. As you can see in the photo, this creates a very blotchy unattractive looking blonde.

This is a prime example of someone who is just trying to overload the hair with colour. She would have been better just lightening the hair to a softer blonde and once her hair had grown adding lighter pieces. This would have been more flattering and worked more harmoniously on her hair.

Renée Zellweger

Recently I've just witnessed Renée Zellweger going back dark. But looking at her natural skin tones, her real colour is certainly towards the blonde. On some photographs she carries it well – when it's well-groomed and styled – but other times I've seen it when it doesn't look right. It's almost as if she trying to get away from what she's got. We all have a tendency to do that. Renée is so much prettier blonde. She carries the dark best when she is dressed in those fantastic evening gowns, with the make-up professionally done to suit much darker tones. And so she should look good – she's a pretty girl. She's a natural blonde, however. Most definitely.

She clearly feels that at the top of her profession, she doesn't need to pander to anyone or anything, be it directors, producers or trends and that she has the power to choose her own hair colour and style. This is the power of super celebrity.

There is another element to that. Actresses of the stature of RZ enjoy being trend setters and to have other women trying to emulate their style. ***Every once in a while, they come up with something radically different and out of character just so that they can watch the world follow suit. There is power in this, too.***

Emma Thompson

I've seen Emma Thompson with lighter hair and she looked pretty, but on this particular picture, the has been bleached and toned out – it is simply dreadful. The first thing that you have to remember is that when you do bleach your hair this substantially you lose your outline, to the point where one can almost see the scalp, especially if your hair is naturally fine. Thompson is almost looking bald, she's become all face – there's just no framing round the face. I am sure she would be the first to admit this was a bad hair day.

Jordan

Actually, I think that Jordan is so pretty, absolutely stunning that, in terms of colour, she can get away with wearing anything and, for that matter, nothing, as well. She certainly, when it comes to hair colour has a great deal of fun with her hair. Her own hair on this picture has been bleached. She's at the stage where it's grown out. A large percentage of the time, Jordan uses hair extensions to change the length and colour of her hair. These are more often than not placed under her parting and behind her hairline. Her own natural hair would then fall on top of the extensions giving the illusion it was her own.

She usually pays a little more attention to creating this illusion than is evident in the photograph.

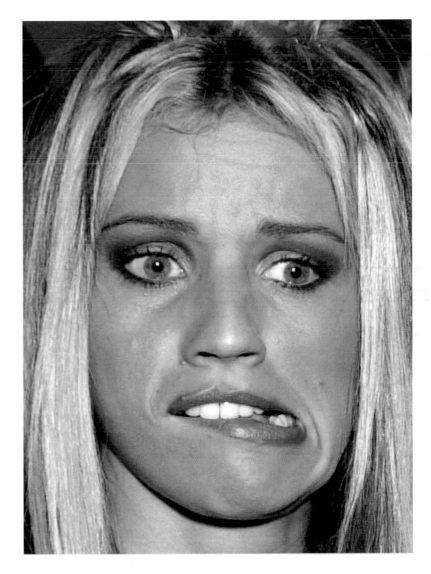

Lisa Marie Presley

Awful! You see again when someone's got naturally dark hair, there's only certain levels of lightness you can achieve and look pretty. It is obvious to me in this picture that her own hair colour when lightened has produced some very brassy tones. To neutralise this, the hair has been toned and in this case, excessively, producing very flat, drab colour.

Cher Wigs, wigs and more wigs.

Madonna

I've never been a big fan of Madonna. I never disliked her, I've just never really been a big fan of hers. I think she's a very clever woman, though. When a woman changes her look as much as she does, I think it's fantastic she's actually managed to stay on top.

Madonna is now in her 40s, so she's got to be getting some grey in the hair. This may well be the reason for an all-over blonding with highlights going just through the top section. That's why you're getting this slightly darker partial kind of tonal, which I think is quite attractive. A tonal difference is what the majority of women look for these days.

I've really seen her hair look better than that. Do you know who wears this colour and style very well in this day and age? Absolutely fantastic. Gwen Stefani.

Gwen Stefani

If there's any woman who absolutely takes the prize for blondeness, it is her. She just sells it so well.

The one who sells it worst today, in my opinion, is Christina Aguliera.She looks absolutely diabolical with her hair.
Courtney Love sells it trampy, Gwen Stefani sells it classy.

There are out there very few people who carry excessive blondeness very well – mostly, it makes hair look just awful when you bleach it that light. Excessive blondness then becomes a whole package - the hair may not look fantastic on some people but when it packages together, they may be able to carry it all off.

Guy Ritchie

Guy Ritchie is one of those people who's naturally got quite fairish hair or, if he hasn't, it seems as if he has been highlighted a little. Whatever he has had done, I don't think it's high maintenance.

Looking at him, on the picture that you're showing, if he were to get more substantial length to his hair, it would get quite light.

You see most men keep their hair short, the only people who don't are the surfer dudes and that's why they get that natural evolution where their hair gets bleached out by the sun. Obviously, most men keep their hair shorter so they don't have to worry about sun discoloration.

Shane Ritchie

Awful. How many men do you know who bleach their hair and wear it well? I've never really taken to men colouring their hair. Occasionally, I see a man who wears it well, but in general, less is more.

John Galliano

His hair is naturally quite dark. I think he's got naturally curly hair, too, so the reason why a lot of this will look bedraggled is because it's been blow-dried straight. What you see on this picture is just a substantial build up of highlights of bleach.

In terms of hair colouring for men, blonde is somewhat more acceptable than red, say, but I've never been a great supporter of it – I feel that for a guy's hair, the minimum of highlights, if he must have any and then, let the sun do the rest to get it just one or two shades lighter.

2004

Kate Winslet

She is a dark blonde, simple as that. It wouldn't surprise me if in this photograph here, a lot of it is her natural hair colour. She perhaps isn't paying a lot of attention to colouring her hair, certainly not in this early photograph.

You've got to remember that when it comes to lightening hair, there's a degree of lightness and also the quantity, certainly when it comes to highlights.
So I would say on this one, she may not be going much too far from her own natural hair colour. But you can see by the lengths if her hair the evolution has lightened it somewhat.

You can see on the mid-length and ends through there already, there's certainly much more colouring going on here.

1997

is Kate in 2004: much
der... and it's very striking,
ugh it could have done with
a little bit more tones going
ugh it. The one thing you
to remember about this
ur is that it will have evolved
a series of highlighting
cations over a period of
. This would not have been
eved by one highlight
cation.

Marilyn Monroe

She was at her most glamorous in *Some Like It Hot*. I think she did have natural fairness to her hair, I don't think she was as dark as she was made out to be.

When you say Marilyn Monroe, the first thing you think about is her blonde hair. This is totally her signature colour. That was to remain with her for the rest of her life. To this day if you mention name Marilyn Monroe you instantly think of the colour of her hair.

This one is a good example of her natural hair. She was a red-head, pure and simple.

I think she always knew when she was Marilyn Monroe (blonde) and when she was Norma Jean (red).

Joanna Lumley

I find this colour a little too flat for Joanna Lumley. I think she would benefit from a fractionally warmer base blonde and adding some lighter highlights to this to give her the lightness she obviously likes. This would be a lot more flattering for her skin tones and benefiting from some much needed dimension to her hair colour. And it's a shame, she's a beautiful woman, and the poor colouring draws the eye even more – because she is so striking.

Jennifer Aniston

If ever anyone's career has benefited from their hair style and colour, it is Jennifer Aniston. The amazing thing is, I don't think she planned it. I don't think she's ever been out there trying to say, 'emulate me, copy me'. Whereas Victoria Beckham is constantly changing her image and would like to be copied, although no one seems to copy her.

Jennifer Aniston has gone from someone who's been quite plain to someone glamorous. And it's obviously happened after she got the blonde hair. I think at one point she did have hair extensions, when she cut her hair very short, but this was short-lived until her own hair grew. She's the quintessential highlights model!

I'll give Jennifer her dues, she only used extensions once. I think she she wanted to be in her own hair, her natural hair.

On this photograph, so much more of the tones come out and the different blondes as well, which I think is quite attractive. And if you look at it closely, this hair coming over her shoulder which is from the back, is darker. We've got the left hand side here where the projection of the blonde is coming more onto the top. But underneath where it's sitting on her shoulder, that is quite dark. It's highlights, it's definitely highlights, over a degree of time. And this is a woman who's looked after her hair, she's very careful. She's not got the blonde anorexic thing where she's had too much done too quickly. She most probably has not even aimed to achieve this – it's just the way it's happened.

1997

I'm not liking it all only for the simple reason that every time I'm looking at her it's almost like a black swimming cap on her head.

If ever anyone's career has benefited from her hair style and colour, it is Jennifer Aniston. The amazing thing is, I don't think she planned it.

Geri Halliwell

Here the hair's just been put through hell – it looks like worms just stuck onto her head, and the fringe is just hanging on for dear life. I think Geri would agree she's had better hair days than on this picture.

She's back to more of a natural hair colour. She's got some highlights in it but it's obviously not as aggressively blonde. These would be hair extensions again.

Part of it is her natural hair colour, and the rest hair extensions.

Kate Moss

Kate Moss' hair colour is naturally quite fair. She has that borderline colour that can remain quite mousy or taken very blonde. The ideal base colour to change when the mood takes you, as not too long ago Kate Moss sported a very blonde look that she carried so well. In the picture, that wouldn't have taken a lot to achieve, to get that blonde…

I get the impression that Kate Moss does not necessarily pay a lot of attention to lightening her hair or, at least, isn't into a high maintenance program. Just a quick balayage, now and again and a few highlights here and there are enough to achieve the look.

Donatella Versace

This is a prime example of pre-lighten and tone. While I hate the colour, I would have my reservations about changing it.

Once in a while you come across a client whose colour makes you suicidal. It not so much that the colour is so ghastly, but what happens when you persuade them to let you change it.

After you've re-coloured it, you spend the next five hours restoring it to what it was.

Some clients have lived so long with what they have got, they really can't change. I suspect that Donatella would be such a client.

Sigourney Weaver
Again, this is done too light. The first thing that happens when lightening much darker hair, as in the Julia Roberts scenario, is that it goes all brassy.
To combat this, bleach highlights are put into the hair. This is most certainly the case here, producing a very flat type of blonde, resembling a wig.

Jemima Goldsmith
She may have had some very soft highlights put in of one or two shades lighter. Not enough to actually notice a difference, but once her hair has been coloured, that hair will become susceptible, through evolution and sunshine, and obviously shampooing and blow-drying, to becoming even lighter.

Naomi Campbell

Is she faking it or making it?
Faking it.

Linda Evangelista

She was the first model to come around where the agency didn't tell her what colour her hair should be. It was her signature to change her hair colour. I think one time she was even blonde, but it wasn't a very good blonde. She went from a blonde to a brunette…so I think she was the first one to come out and have a signature like that. What you've got to remember with hair colour is that it doesn't matter what they say is in fashion, it will always remain individual to the woman.

With hair colour, you can say certain things are in fashion but I think if a woman is a blonde, she will wait for blonde to come in. She will not go brunette.

Normandie Keith

Normandie has her hair lifted up to the blonde that you see. The difference between a high quality blonde and a bad blonde is the extra mile. It's not just doing the roots – with Normandie, it's a matter of several tones of blondes and deeper tones of blonde to give her hair a multi-dimensional look as you can see in the photo.

The difference between a high quality blonde and a bad blonde is the extra mile.

Donna Air

She has highlights – she's been in to the salon – although she might be an all-over hair colour now because she's looking very gingery. I saw recently one of her pictures and I think she may be an all-over tint now.

Jerry Hall

I think she's more or less all-over hair colour now. I would say she's most probably a natural medium blonde, I wouldn't say she's naturally that light. Looking at her hair everyone would think she's quite blonde because she's got masses of hair, but it still has quite a lot of warm tone in it, which tells me that she's quite darkish…

Jennifer Lopez

Obviously she's not a blonde. On a number of pictures she appears I have noticed her hair colour to be much fairer than she could naturally achieve. It would not surprise me if this has not been digitally enhanced to three shades lighter than it actually is. This is highly misleading for young girls of the same colouring who see these shots and aspire to achieve that look.

Occasionally, one catches a more realistic picture from a tabloid or a magazine and sees the true colour of her hair which is warmer and more golden than it appears in the glossy ads she does.

I have observed this chameleon-like change in Lopez's pictures and come to the conclusion that when a magazine caters for white readers, she would be digitally made to look fairer. If the bias of a magazine is towards, say Puerto Rican, she would be made to look darker. So, it depends on which audience she is playing to.

I would see her more as a Kelly Brook kind of blonde.

Sophie Dahl

The first thing you notice about her hair is it's got a lot shorter. When hair goes a lot shorter it's easier to get that kind of concentration, colouring it quite quickly to achieve the very blonde effect. It will certainly be easier on the condition of the hair. Hair that is quite long and dark will take quite a bit of punishment. She could have done with a little bit more length to it, just a fraction. There's still a little bit too many layers in it, which doesn't help to build the blonde up. It really is a little bit too much, too blonde.

Nicole Appleton

She used to wear it so well. I remember some old photos. She used to get the right balance of contrast between blonde and dark. It is obvious from this photo that that is no more. The top blonde is too solid, too extreme and the back so dark. *There seems to be no continuity between these colours – they just seem to be at war.* That just looks like a council estate – awful.

Kelly Brook

Her hair is very very dark naturally, building up to different degrees of lightness which has most certainly been achieved over a period of time. You can see the building up of different tones into the hair, different degrees of blondeness. This is hair that's gone through the elements of change.

This is a classic look. Cat Deeley recently had it, but lost it when she pushed her hair too far. I like this look a lot. Kelly really pulls it off.. A lot of women would go for this one and I think if you have got very very dark hair, but done under controlled circumstances, you can achieve it.

Rebecca Loos

This is a prime example of someone using a few highlights that are 2 to 3 shade lighter than their natural base colour. This is the soft caramel tones that are very complimentary to her hair. Over time, these would most probably lighten just a little more. Ideal for a low maintenance blonde.

Julia Roberts

This colour has most definitely been achieved by pre-lightening and toning the hair. Julia's natural colour, if lightened by hair colour, would have produced a more brassy looking blonde. To keep this colour shown in the photo would be very high maintenance. Whatever the claims on her time and purse, she wears it well.

I personally feel that she should have just stuck to that fabulous coppery blonde that was emanating from her natural colour even adding a small amount of highlights using hair colour alone to emphasise this even more. This to me is most certainly the Julia Roberts' signature hair colour.

1994

SHAUN PULFREY

Mary J. Blige.

Mary J. Blige is someone within the black community I've always found in terms of hair quite interesting. For starters, this is not her own hair. If you look very closely, you'll see the hairline has been sectioned off, with a substantially lighter outline going around it. This may be hard to detect at first glance, but a practised eye can see it. The hair itself would be quite short. Once a bleached hairline is created, longer blonde weaves are stitched on to the existing hair. Once this process is finished, the hairline is pushed back. And when you look at it, it's almost as if it's a natural head of hair. No Afro hair could be bleached that light and straightened and still be on that person's head.

Is it possible to get afro hair absolutely completely blonde all over? **No.**

Most of the time. weaves are used in Afro-hair. This gives them the ability to change colour and length that their own hair could never do. While this can be fun, it can also be expensive. Sometimes, real hair and fake hair is used for these weaves. There a lot of Afro-women who are very skilled at these weaves, even though they are not hairdressers.

Sienna Miller

Without doubt she would seem to have it all. Sienna's colour looks amazing — from the first time I saw her I knew she is one girl who is destined to spend her life as a blonde. No matter how many times she may change it, I am sure she will always go back to blonde. Sorry to say this, girls, but judging by the colour of her natural base colour her hair was just born for blonding. Some girls have all the luck.

Goodbye Jennifer, hello Sienna.

Blondorexia

The syndrome starts out with a client having her hair lightened one or two shades lighter. Within a short space of time she decides to go a little bit blonder. You just know this is only the start. Before long, she will be back in your chair demanding, *I wannabe blonder*. By this time, she has stopped listening to you about the maintenance for her hair... this no longer matters. Her fixation is just to go blonder.

I know I have lost a client to blondorexia when they ask me to blonde their hair way beyond what I consider to be in their best interests. My allegiance is to the client but her hair is my priority.

You warn them against it, but they insist. There is no reasoning with a blondorexic. Even when the toll in terms of time and money becomes exorbitant, they persist. If you send them away, they find another colourist.

When it comes to blonde hair, or should we say lighter hair, it can get too blonde. When women develop blondorexia, they become as light in the head as the hair. If you care for them more than their hair, you stop being their hairdresser and become their therapist.

I call it the hairdresser's couch.

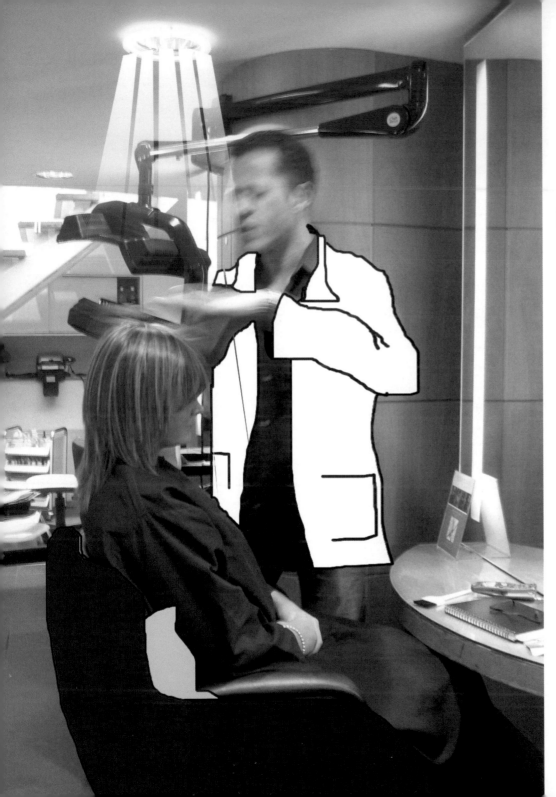

The hairdresser's couch

London, New York and Los Angeles blondes

LONDON BLONDES

There are two types of London blondes: the first is very comfortable with creating her own signature blonde and maintaining it. She is normal. The second, however, is more influenced by the media and TV regarding her hair colour than what her hairdresser or her inner voice tells her is *her*. She is not abnormal, but neither is she normal. She is an in-betweenie.

She believes with a passion that if she is blonder – like whoever – she will become mistress of the universe or find love everlasting. When she doesn't, she assumes it was because she wasn't blonde enough. The solution is blonder.

Money doesn't matter as they pursue their idée fixe. But of course it

does, as even when they are rich there is always some accounting body overseeing their spending. These women have broken too many credit card limits and overdrawn too many bank accounts to exist in an unpoliced financial neverland. Such women are every colourist's potential receivership as they are both blondorexic and 10th dans at running up credit.

The London blonde doesn't mind being considered dumb – she'll toy with it, she'll play smart and dumb. She's up for a laugh more even to the point when she can overdo the fake tan.

Typically, the London blonde would go straight for *HELLO!* magazine and the glossies checking the celebrities' latest hair colours and I would personally say they can, more often than not, influence their choice. They seem more aware of what everyone else is wearing, what everyone else is doing, but they'll tend to have their own little bit of individuality themselves. And once in a while we can share something very intimate, but that's between me and them.

L.A.
Blondes

LOS ANGELES BLONDES

Without question they are *the* competitive blondes.

The LA blonde can never be too blonde and is constantly checking out the competition even amongst her friends. The LA blonde tends to flit between colourists, constantly singing their praises along the way. She loves boasting to friends how amazing her colourist is, implying that her colourist is better than theirs in an almost child-like fashion.

LA is the birthplace of blonde-envy. Our LA blonde is always checking other blondes to see who is blonder. Most aspire to be very blonde – there are few medium and deeper blondes in LA and they are considered brunettes. Whatever you do in LA do not mention the word brassy to a woman as she will have a heart attack. Don't even think of adding warmer tones to her already very blonde hair – she would only feel they make her hair darker. Mention adding complimentary warmer honey tones to a LA blonde and she would give you the look of death

and in an icy tone tell you, 'Darling, I had honey on my toast this morning I think that's enough honey for one day.'

A vast proportion of women in LA try to buy into the blonde look even if they cannot afford it. Some will end up with cheap imitations, that's how desperate they can become to join the only female club.

LA is also the birthplace of the combination blonde: darker-haired women whose hair, after lightening, will always look brassy due to the red pigment in their natural colour. To deal with this, they will proceed to overload the hair with as many highlights as possible to become the cooler looking blonde. The end result is extremely high maintenance and a neurotic colourist.

When they get their good hair days, they can be seen working Rodeo Drive where their set is cruising up and down in open top sports car, vying for a prime table on a sidewalk restaurant and a new beau. All in all this makes for great entertainment. After all, LA *is* the entertainment capital of the world – what else would one expect?!

NEW YORK BLONDES

NY is home to the power and society blonde. They may be different but ultimately both command respect... or else.

Never ever treat a New York power blonde like the stereotype dumb blonde. She will humiliate you with the kind of wit that would get Tom Wolfe scribbling in his notepad, then will proceed to hound you out of a job by pulling the sort of corporate strings that would make even Bill Gates twitch. Don't mess with Miss NY Blonde.

The society blonde has a different kind of rank. There are many American families whose name gives them instant recognition and respect – they may not have titles but to other Americans they are America's own royalty. Their female high-groomers are the classiest blondes in the world.

While the LA blonde will most definitely be flirtatious and project herself in a very sexual way to get what she wants, the New York blonde would never be so blatant or obvious. Even if she were to portray herself thus, it would be in a discreet way.

The society blonde knows she is glamorous and sexy but it is all about class – she would never be seen to be the hunter, always the hunted, yet will relish all the attention she gets. The New York blonde takes herself seriously and will always give it to you straight. My relationship with her was fantastic because she is very knowledgeable about hair colour and knows her limitations and what suits her.

So if you can deliver the goods she would adore you. The first time you get to do a new client she will be watching you like a hawk. She can spot in an instant if you know what you are doing and, if you show any signs of fear or she thinks you are not capable of doing the job, she will zap you. She demands only the highest quality and only the most celebrated colourist will do.New York is the home to some of the biggest celebrity salons in the US and a top colourist can make or break a salon. It is not uncommon for a top New York colourist to charge $500 and upwards. These prices will then become public knowledge and affordable to only the very few.

The New York blonde tends to prefer tones on the lighter side (not the stronger contrasts of their British counterparts) but she has the ultimate price on her head – hair that states I am rich and classy. That price will come with the salon's name, ultimately labelling her hair just like the labels that are stitched to her clothes.

New York blondes tend to be quite private – they do not reveal too much about themselves till you have gained their trust. The utmost discretion is expected from their colourist and the confidences of the hairdresser's chair are inviolate... or else.

The power of the *blonde*

Never under-estimate the power of a blonde. I have seen it used in many different ways... for revenge on a cheating partner to enticing a potential partner as a husband to deflecting an investigation by the Inland Revenue. Men are bewitched by the glamorous blonde and never more strongly did I witness this than during my time in Los Angeles. Show me a woman who made it big time in LA who isn't blonde.

This is real feminism, blonde in tooth and claw. These are women who are go-getting with every weapon they can muster, and blonde is basic to the armoury that makes men go weak at the knees. They also see the up-coming blonde competition and try to take it out with all the finesse of a mafia Donatella. The right-placed smear in an on-side gossip column can, career-wise, be just as fatal as a hitman's bullet. This is not blonde-envy so much as blonde wars. Needless to say, a good colourist in LA is worth his weight in blonde bars.

Changing your colour will
change your life

How much do women expect from being blonde can vary considerably. Certainly, in Los Angeles the blonde expects a high return for her investment. The rich husband and constant attention, fame ultimately being the icing on the cake. English blondes – while a few may have LA blonde ball-busting aspirations – are rather more genteel: much calmer, less demanding than their American counterpart and, all round, just less ballsy. I think it would be true to say they will change if they were to trade places. Hopefully, they won't... while the world needs more blonde, it has definitely got all the testosterone it needs.

I've never had a client whose hair colour I didn't want to change.

Shaun Pulfrey
www.shaunpulfrey.com

Acknowledgements

With special thanks to:

My brother Glyn for taking the pressure off me when I left school and followed in the family business.

My biggest fan and best (blonde) sister a brother could wish for, Kerry, for keeping me on my toes all these years

All the old school chums from Vidal Sassoon`s – it was an amazing time and their support and training has carried me so well through all these years and continues to this day.

Annie Humphreys, head of colour and technical research at Vidal Sassoon`s for giving me, this 21-year-old northern lad, the opportunity of a lifetime. You were and still are an inspiration to this day. On behalf of all the colour technicians who have had the honour to be taken under your wing…you are without question the true queen of colour.

The entire team at Richard Ward's for putting up with me day in and day out and my constant gabbing on about the book. Thanks for listening, you guys are the best.

Richard and Helen Ward for giving me the opportunity to prove myself… my eternal gratitude.

Valentina at Artnik without whom this would not have been possible…for the changes you have inspired in me. Without question women bring out the best in me and you are no exception.

Michael in Boston for putting up with me for six years during which it must have seemed that the world revolved around hair colour.

Nigel for his support and friendship over the years – from the days in Hulme till now… I never dreamt it would get this far. From the bottom of my heart and with all my love for all you have done for me.

And finally, all the women I have ever coloured.

a passion to make women look great. I believe I satisfy all these conditions.

I have written this book not for other professional colourists but for their clients. I want women to know what I know, so they understand what colourists can can do and, more importantly, should be doing. When I started hairdressing I began to look at women's hair colour on the streets and was shocked to see that one colour stood out by far as the worst. Blonde. On close examination I could see that they were not all home dyes either, but there were some bad hair colourists out there.

This book has been inspired by my continued passion for hair and is dedicated to all you hairdressers who share this passion. Keep up the good work – it seems there are a few who do not and the client is getting short-changed, and nothing upsets me more than to see this.

This is not as goody-two-shoes as it sounds. If this book is widely-read I might spend more of my time colouring women's hair well, rather than repairing the mess other colourists have made of it.

Shaun Pulfrey
Senior Technician

blondes: she is not dumb... nor is she naturally blonde. But why blonde?

Gentlemen Prefer Blondes is both a bit of folk wisdom and a '50s' film, staring Marilyn Monroe – incidentally the one where she sings 'Diamonds are a girls' best friend'. But there is actually a bit of science behind the claim that men prefer blondes. The reason they do is that light coloured-hair highlights the face and makes the eyes look more dilated than dark hair. Dilated pupils are a subliminal signal of interest. It doesn't work the other way as, where women are concerned, men seem permanently dilated; consequently women find more discriminatory signals to respond to... like the ability to buy those diamonds.

> *The reason they do is that light coloured-hair highlights the face and makes the eyes look more dilated than dark hair. Dilated pupils are a subliminal signal of interest. It doesn't work the other way as, where women are concerned, men seem permanently dilated; consequently women find more discriminatory signals to respond to... like the ability to buy those diamonds.*

Lightening the hair, then, is part of the female business of attracting the male. And more and more women are doing it. This is not because they are trying harder to attract the men but because we are richer, living longer, striving to look younger, and the products for wannabe blondes are becoming more sophisticated. We have more resources and time for grooming or in a minor way, I suppose, helping along the reproduction of the species.

Yet, in my view, at a time when there is more demand for their services the colourists are not as skillful as they were. I spend a lot of time in my salon clearing up the mess other so-called colourists have made of some of their erstwhile clients' hair. Colouring is an extremely subtle, complex and, not to put too fine a point on it, hair-splitting skill that calls for flair, a long apprenticeship and

The job with Sassoon was a six-month colour programme. I completed it in three. By the early '80s I was working for Vidal on Sloane Street as a colourist and spent the following four years there. From there I went to San Francisco, then onto New York. I thought I was fast until I worked in New York, but there I became even faster. I liked NY women – if you worked well and fast, there was no problem.

I spent just over a year New York and, then, I moved to the blondest city on earth, Los Angeles. They even have photographs of when they were six months old to prove they are naturally blonde. LA also has the highest concentration of people trained in Adobe Photoshop on the planet. In hairdressing terms, LA was the loudest wake up call since I'd joined Vidal Sassoon. It is very, very tough, but I think I helped make it a more interestingly blonder city.

The salon itself was like a stage – a theatrical or movie set – with every hairdresser vying for famous clients. Faye Dunaway used to pop in quite a lot. She came into the London salon, too, and I liked her. I remember her making a comment one time on the differences between America and England:

> *In America they always love the rising star;*
> *in England they love the falling star.*

I always remember it – a smart comment. If you asked Faye what is the capital of California, she might say 'C' because she'd be sending you up. Faye is blonde but she is not dumb. In fact, Faye is like most

I chose Manchester because I knew that I could get a basic training there in a good salon. I chose well and, in the late 70s I served my apprenticeship in just under three years.

After a year in Manchester I was colouring hair, which was what I also knew I wanted to do. At that time, hair colourists were secondary to cutters but I quickly realised that while cut was important colour was vital.

Towards the end of my apprenticeship a friend of mine who was a hair colourist asked me if there was a job for him at the salon. I told him I'd seen Vidal Sassoon was looking for hair colourists to hire in London. I remember giving him all the details and then thinking to myself: 'My God, I should be doing that. I shouldn't be sending him there, *I* should be going.'

So I sent my details off and, in 1981, went for an interview. After a couple more interviews, and a few white lies about my aunt living in London (and how I could live with her), I got the job. Sassoon had a very, very good programme for training hair colourists. In fact, they were perhaps one of the first in London to differentiate between colourists and cutters.

The main hurdle was getting comfortable with the idea of living in London. It was easier then than now, as we could fiddle our tube fares a little bit, and manage to keep a bit more of our slaves' wages in our pocket.

Preface

I grew up in a fishing town called Grimsby, on the Lincolnshire coast. My family were in fishing, and in school everyone was destined either for the trawlers or to help in the processing of the catch.

As a pupil, I didn't apply myself that well because I was always much better with my hands. I would babysit for my next door neighbour who was a hairdresser. She would leave a lot of the hairdressing books around and I'd look at the books. I knew from that moment what I wanted to be.

But my father wanted me to be a fisherman. He wanted me to join the family business, so quite often he took me out fishing, sometimes for three weeks at a time. I did it to show I could do it if I had to. But I knew I didn't have to, and that I wouldn't. My Dad had pushed me so hard towards something I had no interest in that I became all the more determined to do what I wanted – hairdressing.

But he could see I had no interest in fishing, and in the end he just said, 'You've got to do it how you want.'

I started in my home town and within a very short time I knew I had made the right choice. I was there for about a year before moving on to Manchester. I gave the location a great deal of thought: If I'd set off for London first, people mightn't have taken me seriously, they would have thought, 'Yeah, alright, really you want the bright lights!'

To my **Mum**
With all my love

I wannabe
BLONDE

Shaun Pulfrey
CELEBRITY HAIR COLOURIST

artnik

First published in Great Britain in 2005
by Artnik
341b Queenstown Road
London SW8 4LH
UK

ISBN 1-903906-58-X

Design: Supriya Sahai
Illustrations: Faye Durston
Book Concept: Nicholas Artsrunik
Editor: John McVicar

Printed and bound in Spain by Graficas Diaz

I wannabe
BLONDE